OUT OF THIS WORLD

Meet NASA Inventor Mahmooda Sultana and Her Team's

Quantum Dot Solar Sail

www.worldbook.com

World Book, Inc.
180 North LaSalle Street
Suite 900
Chicago, Illinois 60601
USA

For information about other World Book publications, visit our website at www.worldbook.com or call 1-800-WORLDBK (967-5325).

For information about sales to schools and libraries, call 1-800-975-3250 (United States), or 1-800-837-5365 (Canada).

© 2024 (print and e-book) by World Book, Inc. All rights reserved. No part of this publication may be reproduced, stored in a retrieval system, or transmitted in any form or by any means (electronic, mechanical, photocopying, recording, or otherwise) without written permission from World Book, Inc.

WORLD BOOK and the GLOBE DEVICE are registered trademarks or trademarks of World Book, Inc.

Produced in collaboration with the National Aeronautics and Space Administration (NASA).

Library of Congress Cataloging-in-Publication Data for this volume has been applied for.

Out of This World
ISBN: 978-0-7166-6564-9 (set, hc.)

Quantum Dot Solar Sail
ISBN: 978-0-7166-6571-7 (hc.)

Also available as:
ISBN: 978-0-7166-6579-3 (e-book)
ISBN: 978-0-7166-6587-8 (soft cover)

Staff

Editorial

Vice President
Tom Evans

Senior Manager, New Content
Jeff De La Rosa

Writer
William D. Adams

Editor
Emma Flickinger

Curriculum Designer
Caroline Davidson

Proofreader
Nathalie Strassheim

Indexer
Nathaniel Lindstrom

Graphics and Design

Senior Visual Communications Designer
Melanie Bender

Digital Asset Specialist
Rosalia Bledsoe

Acknowledgments

Cover	NASA	22-23	JAXA
3	NASA/JPL/USGS; JAXA	24-25	© naratrip/Shutterstock
4-5	© Mark Garlick, Science Source	26-27	NASA
6-7	NASA Ames/JPL-Caltech	28-29	NASA/Pat Izzo; © Eric Broder Van Dyke, Shutterstock
8-9	© Mark Garlick, Science Source	30-31	© Leo Matyushkin, Shutterstock
10-11	Mahmooda Sultana	33	Mahmooda Sultana
12-13	NASA/JPL/USGS	34-35	NASA
14-15	© Science Photo Library/Alamy Images	36-37	© Digital Images Studio/Shutterstock
17	Mahmooda Sultana	38-39	© Artsiom P/Shutterstock
18-19	NASA	40-41	© Vadim Sadovski, Shutterstock
20-21	© amgun/Shutterstock	42-43	© Jurik Peter, Shutterstock
		44	© Massachusetts Institute of Technology

Contents

- 4 Introduction
- 8 Voyager 2 explores Uranus and Neptune
- 10 INVENTOR FEATURE: Early life
- 12 Triton: Pluto's sibling
- 14 Is Triton habitable?
- 16 INVENTOR FEATURE: Defying expectations
- 18 The closing window to study Triton's poles
- 20 Radiation pressure
- 22 Solar sails
- 24 Spectroscopy
- 26 In search of a smaller spectrometer
- 28 Quantum dots
- 30 BIG IDEA: Quantum dot spectrometer
- 32 INVENTOR FEATURE: Goddard and hobbies
- 34 BIG IDEA: Quantum dot spectrometer on a solar sail
- 36 Supercharged solar sailing
- 38 Beating the heat
- 40 Expanding the SCOPE
- 42 Learning about exoplanets through the ice giants
- 44 Defying expectations
- 45 Glossary
- 46 Review and reflect
- 48 Index

Glossary There is a glossary of terms on page 45. Terms defined in the glossary are in boldface type that **looks like this** on their first appearance on any spread (two facing pages).

Pronunciations (how to say words) are given in parentheses the first time some difficult words appear in the book. They look like this: pronunciation (pruh NUHN see AY shuhn).

Introduction

Humans have sent dozens of space probes to Mars, including all kinds of **orbiters, landers, rovers,** and even a helicopter! But, how many spacecraft have been sent to Uranus and Neptune? Just one. The same craft passed by both planets in a brief flyby mission.

Mars is certainly interesting enough to warrant all that attention. But part of the problem is that it is much more technically challenging, time-consuming, and expensive to reach the outer four planets of the **solar system.**

It took the Voyager 2 spacecraft, launched in 1977, eight years to reach Uranus and four more years after that to reach Neptune. No probe has since visited either planet because of the daunting distance.

An artist's illustration of Voyager 2 approaching Uranus

Nevertheless, scientists and engineers are now determined to revisit these ice giants. In doing so, we will discover more about our own **solar system,** of course. But we will learn more than that. Most of of the **exoplanets** (planets beyond our solar system) that have been discovered so far are about the size of Neptune. We can apply what we learn about our own ice giants to other planetary systems.

Mahmooda Sultana, an instrument scientist at the Goddard Space Flight Center (GSFC) near Washington, D.C., wants to use a high-tech **propulsion** system that harnesses the power of sunlight to reach distant targets in record time. But, while such technology is limited in what it can carry, Mahmooda has an idea to greatly reduce the size and **mass** of an important scientific instrument. The resulting probe could make many important science measurements, but it would get there in a fraction of the time and at a fraction of the cost of a traditional mission.

The NASA Innovative Advanced Concepts program. The titles in the *Out of This World* series feature projects that have won grant money from a group formed by the United States National Aeronautics and Space Administration, or NASA. The NASA Innovative Advanced Concepts program (NIAC) provides funding to teams working to develop bold new advances in space technology. You can visit NIAC's website at www.nasa.gov/niac.

Meet Mahmooda Sultana.

"I've defied expectations my entire life. Now, I want to defy the expectations of what a small probe to the outer solar system can accomplish, how long it takes to reach its target, and what it costs."

Artist's rendering of an exoplanet system

Voyager 2 explores Uranus and Neptune

In the 1960's, astronomers noticed an approaching alignment in the orbits of the outer four planets of the **solar system:** Jupiter, Saturn, Uranus, and Neptune. For a short time in the 1970's, this alignment would enable a **probe** launched from Earth to fly past all four planets. They also found that such an alignment would not happen again for another 175 years. **Engineers,** mission planners, and policy advisers had to act quickly to take advantage of this once-in-many-lifetimes opportunity.

In response, NASA developed the Voyager program. Two Voyager probes, both launched in 1977, swung from planet to planet, using the **gravitational attraction** of each target to redirect themselves to the next.

Scientists desperately wanted to observe Saturn's large moon Titan, which they thought capable of harboring life. But, Titan was on the wrong side of Saturn for a gravity assist. The Voyager probes could not observe Titan and fly on to Uranus and Neptune. So, NASA split up the probes. Voyager 1 flew by Titan, sacrificing the chance to continue on to Uranus and Neptune. Voyager 2 missed Titan but reached both ice giants.

An artist's illustration of Voyager visiting Neptune

Inventor feature:
Early life

Mahmooda was born in the South Asian country of Bangladesh.

❝ I was always interested in math and science. ❞ —Mahmooda

It seemed that she had science and **engineering** in her blood:

❝ I came from an engineering background. My dad was a civil engineer. My grandfather was an electrical engineer. ❞ —Mahmooda

Civil engineering involves the planning and supervision of such large construction projects as bridges, canals, dams, tunnels, and water supply systems. Electrical

Mahmooda's dad instructing her in chess

engineering involves the development, production, and testing of electrical and electronic devices and equipment.

❚❚ I grew up reading a lot of science-fiction books. Jules Verne's novels were always inspiring to me. I think that might have been the first spark in inspiring me to pursue science and technology. ❚❚ —Mahmooda

Jules Verne (1828-1905) was a French author who wrote some of the first science-fiction stories. Verne's stories forecast the invention of airplanes, television, guided missiles, and space satellites. They were written in the 1800's, decades before such things existed!

Triton:
Pluto's sibling

There's another planet-sized body lurking out there with the two ice giants. Triton is the largest of Neptune's 14 moons. It has a diameter of 1,680 miles (2,700 kilometers), making it one of the largest moons in the **solar system.** It is slightly larger than the **dwarf planet** Pluto.

In fact, Triton shares many similarities with Pluto. Triton likely formed in the **Kuiper belt,** like Pluto. The Kuiper belt is a band of objects in the outer regions of the solar system. Triton could not have formed from material left over from the formation of the planet it orbits, as do most other moons. Scientists know this because Triton **orbits** in the direction opposite that Neptune spins. (As moons form, they develop an orbit that matches the spin of the parent planet.) This means that Triton must have formed elsewhere and been captured by Neptune. Triton probably had a long, oval-shaped orbit, like that of Pluto, before getting captured by Neptune's **gravitational pull.**

Scientists were stunned when Voyager's flyby of Triton revealed a geologically varied world with few craters. The lack of craters suggests that geological processes on Triton continually reshape its surface. The flyby also revealed that Triton has a thin **atmosphere,** just like Pluto.

❞ It has a highly energetic **ionosphere,** even though it's so far away from the sun. ❞ —Mahmooda

❚❚ It's one of the few places in our solar system that's geologically active. ❚❚ —Mahmooda

An ionosphere is the part of an atmosphere that has many electrically charged particles. These particles are produced by cosmic rays and radiation from the sun.

Is Triton habitable?

❝ There are a lot of unknowns still about Triton. But, we know that it has some of the ingredients needed for life. ❞ —Mahmooda

You might not think of the edge of the **solar system** harboring life. But, Triton is an intriguing place to look.

Scientists think Triton may hold an ocean of liquid water under its surface. If such an ocean exists, it might have conditions favorable for life.

Drilling to reach such an ocean would be an extremely challenging endeavor. But Triton itself might blast samples of ocean water into space! Voyager 2 detected dozens of large geysers near Triton's south pole during its flyby.

Scientists suspect that similar geysers might exist near the north pole as well. If the polar geysers are connected to a subsurface ocean, their spray would enable a visiting **probe** to analyze the makeup of the ocean without having to drill down to it.

Because of Triton's unique blend of characteristics, the NASA Outer Planets Assessment Group named it the highest priority target among candidate ocean worlds—places where a subsurface ocean is strongly suspected but not definitively known to exist.

Inventor feature:
Defying expectations

With both a family history and a personal interest in science and **engineering,** it might seem that Mahmooda would have an easy path forward. But, it was not that easy at all!

❝ There were challenges as well! ❞ —Mahmooda

Throughout her life, Mahmooda ran up against other people's expectations about the kind of fields women should be active in.

❝ I was born in Bangladesh. In my culture, there are certain expectations. For example, my family expected me to go into the medical field. They wanted me to be a doctor, and not to go into scientific research and engineering. ❞ —Mahmooda

When Mahmooda was a teenager, she moved with her family to the United States. She continued to feel the pressure of those expectations.

❝ It was not just in Bangladesh. Even in the U.S. in high school, I had seen a difference in expectations. Women aren't expected to go into math and science. Oftentimes, it's unspoken expectations, sort of like social expectations. That can be difficult to get around. ❞ —Mahmooda

But Mahmooda knew she wanted to be involved in science and technology. She persevered in studying those subjects, eventually earning her Ph.D. degree in chemical engineering from the Massachusetts Institute of Technology (MIT).

Mahmooda stands with her father at her graduation from MIT.

The closing window to study Triton's poles

As astronomers found more and more Neptune-sized **exoplanets**, the need to revisit the **solar system's** ice giants became clear. But, the distance and cost continued to stand in the way.

> ❝ Outer solar system exploration is really challenging due to many factors, including high cost—oftentimes it needs to be a multibillion-dollar flagship mission—and the long travel time that often increases cost as well. ❞ —Mahmooda

In the 2010's, NASA planners devised a mission to explore Triton as part of the agency's mid-cost Discovery Program. A craft called Trident was to fly by the moon, getting close enough to sample Triton's wispy atmosphere. But in 2021, NASA officials selected other concepts for the next Discovery missions.

> ❝ Also, the window for implementation of the mission adds more challenges. ❞ —Mahmooda

NASA's passing over of the Trident mission was a disappointment to scientists interested in the outer solar system. Around 2045, Triton will fall out of a special alignment that would enable a flyby **probe** to study both its poles. Owing to Neptune's slow

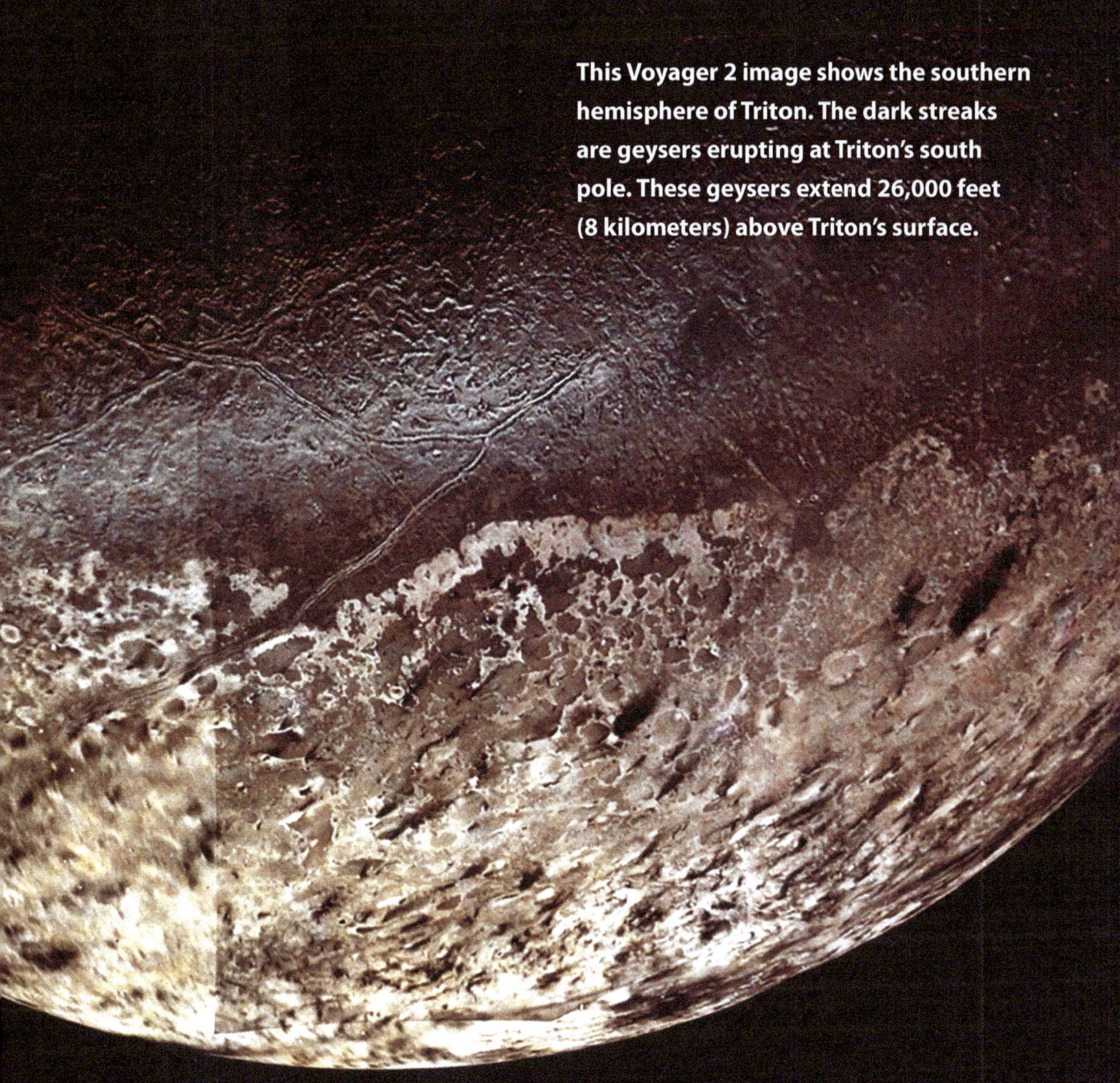

This Voyager 2 image shows the southern hemisphere of Triton. The dark streaks are geysers erupting at Triton's south pole. These geysers extend 26,000 feet (8 kilometers) above Triton's surface.

orbit of the sun, both of Triton's poles will not be *illuminated* (lit up) again for another century. Even if NASA selected Trident or a similar mission in the future, the extended design, construction, and cruise times of a conventional mission would make it hard to get there in time to observe both polar regions.

Radiation pressure

To get to Triton in time to observe its poles and do so on a tight budget, Mahmooda is counting on a strange property of light. Light travels in tiny particles called **photons.** A photon has no **mass.** Mass is the amount of matter an object has. Mass is usually what gives an object **momentum,** or resistance to changing direction or speed. But photons travel so fast that they still have a tiny bit of momentum.

The force exerted by photons striking an object is called **radiation pressure.** The *magnitude* (size) of the force exerted by each photon is tiny. A person standing on Earth's surface cannot feel radiation pressure on their skin. But in space, radiation pressure can affect small bodies—including spacecraft.

Engineers have dealt with such effects for decades. They might have to add extra **propellant** to keep a spacecraft in alignment, for example, because radiation pressure keeps pushing it in a particular direction.

But, spacecraft can also take advantage of radiation pressure. For example, radiation pressure extended the life of the **exoplanet**-finding telescope Kepler. After several reaction wheels—devices used to steer the craft—failed, mission planners used radiation pressure to keep it aligned to search for more exoplanets.

Solar sails

In fact, a spacecraft can be propelled entirely by **radiation pressure.** Such a propulsion system needs no fuel, or even electricity, other than what is needed to power the spacecraft's instruments. Such a propulsion system is called a **solar sail.** Engineers designing solar-sailing spacecraft seek to minimize the craft's **mass** and maximize its surface area.

Even in space, a spacecraft still has mass. Therefore, a more massive spacecraft requires more power to **accelerate** it towards its destination. But solar radiation pressure is fixed as a function of the distance from the sun. So the way to make the most of the available radiation pressure is to make a solar-sailing craft with as little mass as possible.

On Earth, sailing ships with more sail surface area harness more force from the wind. In the same way, a solar-sailing craft with more surface area can harness more force from radiation pressure than a craft with less surface area.

Engineers have developed spacecraft to test the solar sail concept. In 2010, the Japanese **Aerospace** Exploration Agency (JAXA) launched a solar sail demonstration mission called Interplanetary Kite-craft Accelerated by Radiation of the Sun (IKAROS). IKAROS tested several solar sail technologies, including solar sail deployment and steering the craft.

Illustration of the Japanese IKAROS space probe in flight

Spectroscopy

How do scientists know what planets and moons are made of? In most cases, no **probe** has ever sampled their surfaces or clouds. Instead, scientists use a technique called *spectroscopy*.

Such studies are conducted using a device called a spectrometer. Say, for example, a spectrometer analyzes the light coming from the planet Jupiter and finds that it has a particular spectrum. Astronomers can see that the spectrum matches that caused by the absorption of a mixture of pure hydrogen and pure helium. Therefore, they can conclude that the atmosphere mostly contains hydrogen and helium.

Spectroscopy is an incredibly important field of study. In addition to finding the composition of stars, planets, and moons, it is used to create pictures of **molecules,** proteins, and the inner workings of the body.

This is an emission spectrum of the chemical element hydrogen in visible light. If scientists detect such lines from an unknown sample using spectroscopy, they can be sure it contains hydrogen.

❞ If we can separate the different wavelengths, we can figure out what specific wavelength a particular sample absorbs or emits light at. By mapping that out, we can create a signature for a specific sample, be it certain atmospheric components or minerals. ❞ —Mahmooda

In search of a smaller spectrometer

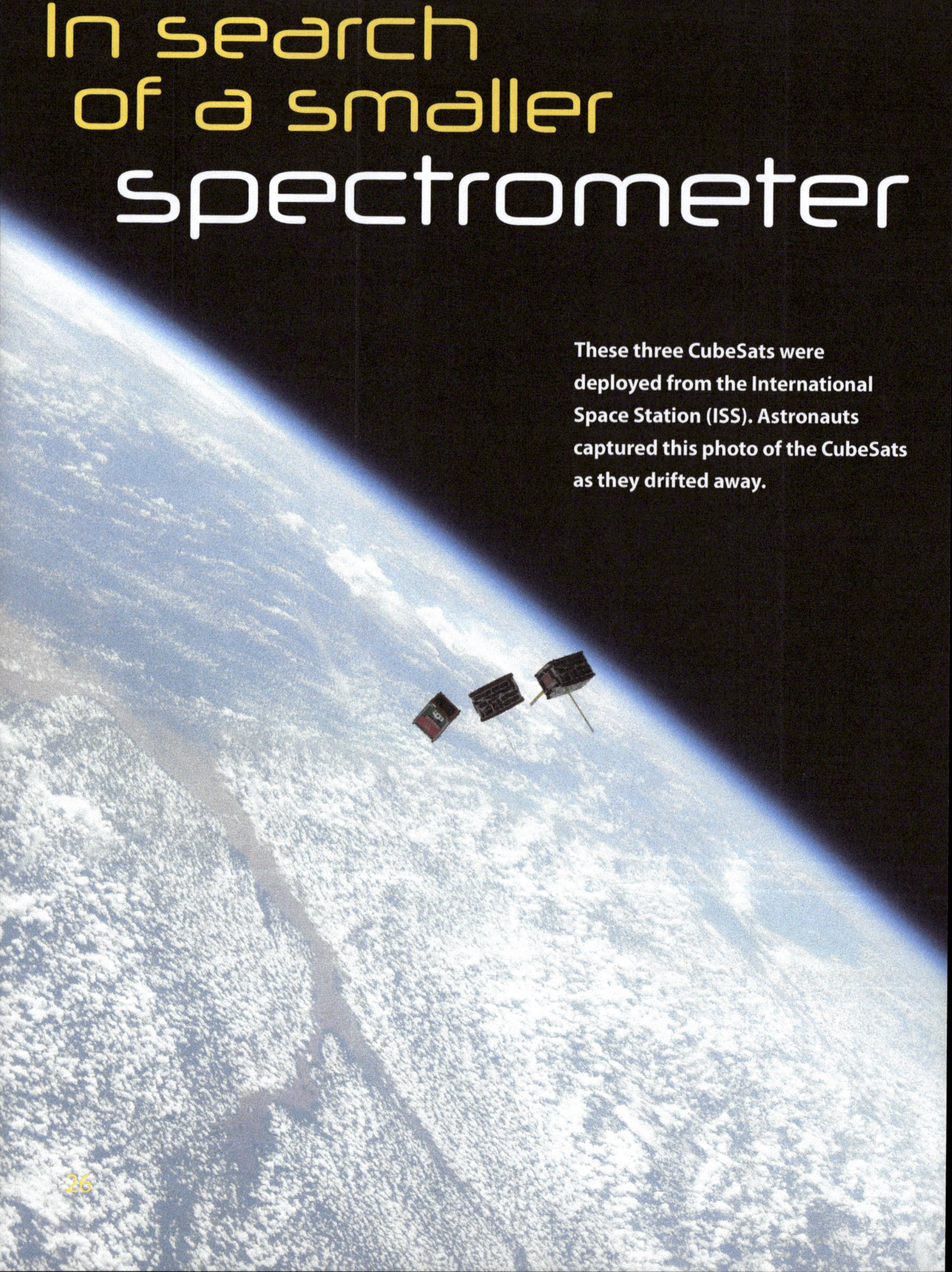

These three CubeSats were deployed from the International Space Station (ISS). Astronauts captured this photo of the CubeSats as they drifted away.

A conventional spectrometer uses a grating or a prism to separate light from a particular source into a spectrum. To produce a high-resolution spectrum, the separated light must travel over a long path. Spectrometers usually have mirrors to create a longer path length. The light then falls on a detector.

The need for a grating or prism, mirrors, and a long path length makes conventional spectrometers large, complicated instruments.

> I first started working on this quantum dot spectrometer idea because I wanted to find something miniaturized enough to fit in a CubeSat. —Mahmooda

CubeSats are a type of small satellite. Mahmooda was working to develop a CubeSat with a spectrometer to study atmospheric conditions on Earth and the sun. A typical CubeSat form factor is about the size of a loaf of bread. But existing spectrometers were simply too large to fit within the strict size constraints of a CubeSat.

Mahmooda began collaborating with Moungi Bawendi, a chemistry professor at the Massachusetts Institute of Technology (MIT). Bawendi is an expert in *synthesizing* (creating) quantum dots. Bawendi was awarded the 2023 Nobel Prize in Chemistry for his work with quantum dots.

Quantum dots

Quantum dots are a form of **nanotechnology.** They are extremely small crystals that can have unique optical or electrical properties. Quantum dots are sometimes called "artificial **atoms,**" because they can have physical properties not normally seen in nature.

A quantum dot is made of dozens of atoms of a *semiconductor*. A semiconductor is a material that conducts electric current better than an insulator like glass, but not as well as a conductor like copper. Scientists can create hundreds of kinds of quantum dots, each with its own special properties.

❞ That allows us to tune the absorption curve by changing size or even shape in some cases of these particles, and of course the composition. This lets us make a set of distinct quantum dot pixels, each having a unique transmission curve. ❞
—Mahmooda

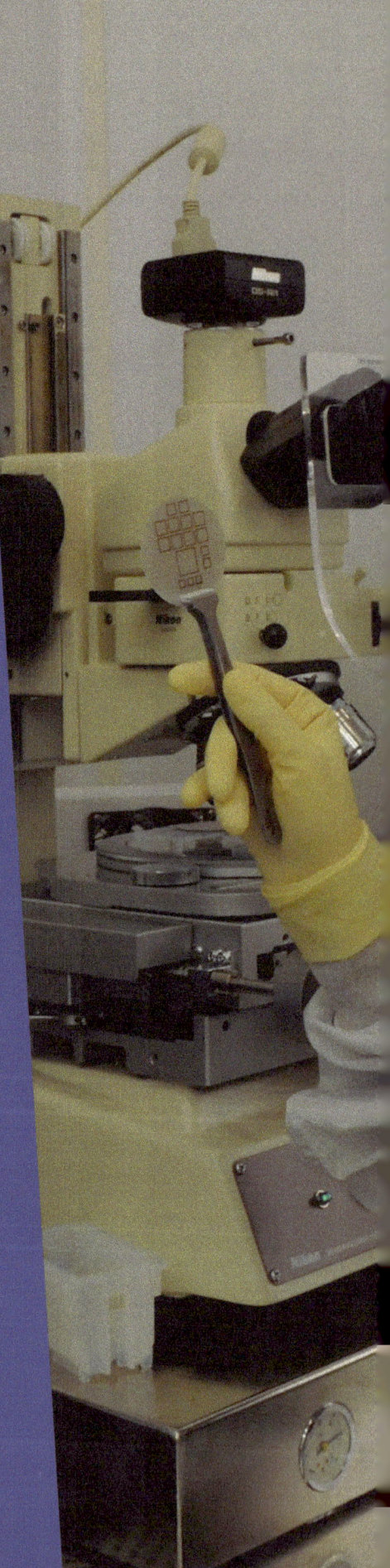

Down to Earth:

Ideas from space that could serve us on our planet.

Quantum dot technology is a rapidly growing field. For example, television manufacturers are including quantum dots in new LED TV's. The LED backlight produces pure blue light. A layer of quantum dots absorbs some of this light and emits red and green light. The quantum dots paired with the blue LED produce a brighter, crisper display than a traditional LED TV, which uses white LED's and filters.

Mahmooda studying nanotechnology materials in the lab for potential uses in spaceflight

Big idea:
Quantum dot spectrometer

In a conventional spectrometer, a prism or grating breaks light into different wavelengths. But if several types of quantum dots that only respond to certain wavelengths could be put together, then they could function as a spectrometer.

> The quantum dot spectrometer is a really interesting idea where we print quantum dots of different sizes, giving a unique optical transmission profile that we can use to make a spectrometer.
> —Mahmooda

A quantum dot spectrometer would be far simpler than conventional designs.

> The beauty of this design is that it eliminates the optical elements needed in a conventional spectrometer, like the grating or prism that usually separates the wavelengths….For those conventional spectrometer ideas, you need a long path length to achieve high spectral resolution…. Because we no longer need that long path length, we can make this a really compact and small spectrometer. —Mahmooda

Glass tubes filled with a quantum dot suspension glow with all colors of the rainbow when exposed to ultraviolet radiation.

Inventor feature: Goddard and hobbies

Mahmooda is an instrument scientist at the Planetary Environments Laboratory within Goddard Space Flight Center (GSFC) near Washington, D.C. It is named after Robert Goddard (1882-1945), an American pioneer of rocket science. GFSC is a NASA research center that develops, builds, and manages science space missions and observatories.

> At Goddard, we are really fortunate to have some amazing scientists and engineers. They are all so smart and hardworking and dedicated to the cause of space science. —Mahmooda

Mahmooda has a variety of hobbies, including playing strategic board games and gardening. She also enjoys sketching and painting.

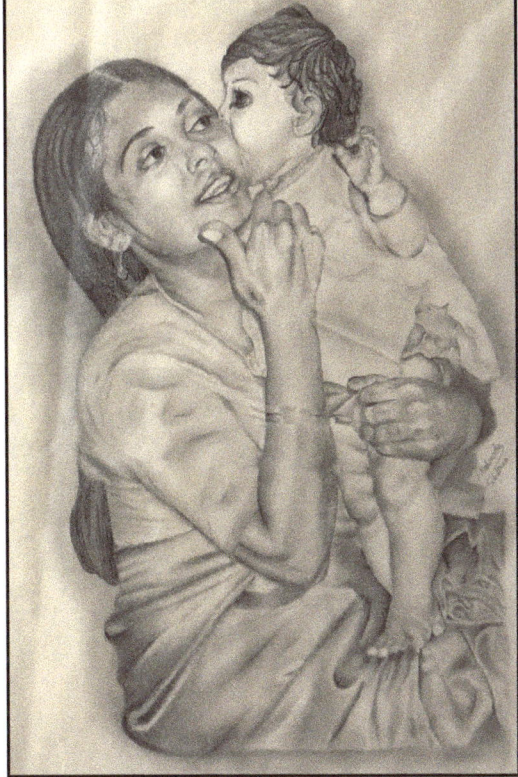

Some of Mahmooda's oil paintings and sketches

Big idea:
Quantum dot spectrometer on a solar sail

Instead of using a quantum dot spectrometer to monitor Earth, Mahmooda had the idea to combine it with a **solar sail** to explore the outer reaches of the **solar system.**

Because a solar-sailing spacecraft must have such a low **mass,** it can have few scientific instruments. But, what if the sail itself could be studded with quantum dots, turning it into a giant spectrometer? The added mass of the quantum dots is very small, even for a solar sail craft.

Mahmooda calls her proposed concept ScienceCraft for Outer Planet Exploration (SCOPE). Her lab is working out the details of this design. First, they showed that they could reliably print the quantum dots onto a solar-saillike film.

❝ We have developed processes to print these quantum dot suspensions in an automated fashion. ❞ —Mahmooda

Another critical step is to test the output of the quantum dot devices from known samples, so that astronomers will be able to tell what SCOPE is looking at.

❞ In my lab, we have figured out a way to characterize the optical transmission curves from these individual pixels. ❞
—Mahmooda

Supercharged solar sailing

To boost SCOPE's speed, Mahmooda and her team plan for it to take a detour around the sun! A conventional rocket will launch the craft from Earth and put it on a path near the sun. As SCOPE nears its closest point to the sun, it will unfurl its **solar sail.** This route takes advantage of several effects caused by being near our star.

1. The sun's **gravitational pull** causes objects that are approaching it to **accelerate.** Therefore, SCOPE would already be moving quickly without the need for any engines.

2. A fast-moving object gains more force from further acceleration than a slow-moving object gains from the same amount acceleration. This is called the Oberth effect, for the German rocket theorist Hermann Oberth.

3. It is very bright near the sun! **Radiation pressure** is directly related to the number of **photons**—or brightness.

Together, these effects will enable SCOPE to scoot to Neptune in five to seven years. At that speed, it could get to the system in plenty of time to observe both of Triton's poles, even if it launched in the late 2030's.

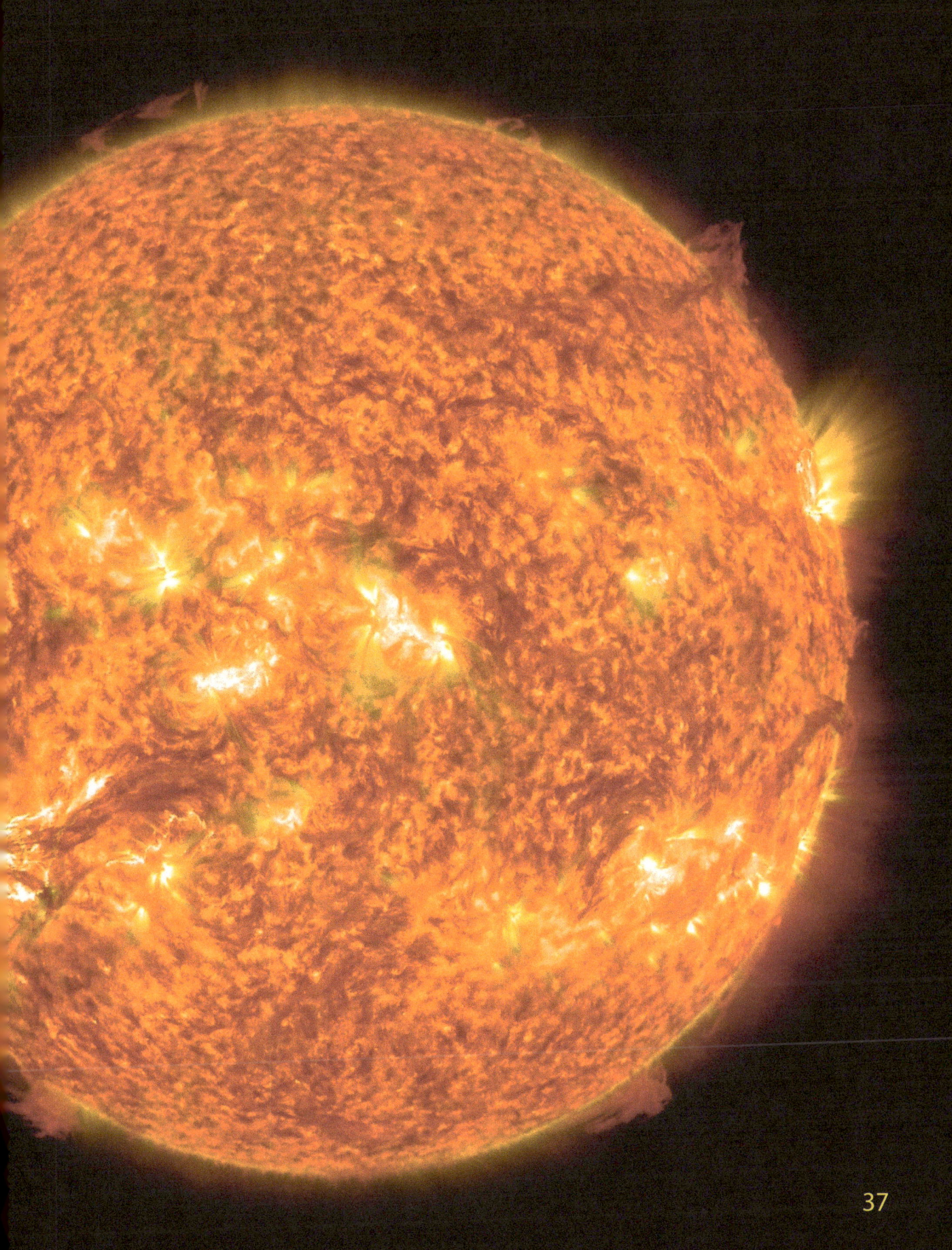

Beating the heat

To achieve this high speed, SCOPE will fly within 30 million miles (50 million kilometers) of the sun—as close as Mercury gets to the sun in its orbit. But, this is not close enough to pose a serious threat to SCOPE's components, with the right design choices.

❝ It turns out that the small temperature increases can be accounted for through materials choice in the sail and the instruments. Our thermal analyses show that our materials choices work well at this distance from the sun. ❞ —Mahmooda

To further test SCOPE's components, Mahmooda's team has arranged for them to be part of a Materials International Space Station Experiment (MISSE). A rocket will fly samples of the quantum dots printed on pieces of solar sail material to the International Space Station (ISS). MISSE samples are mounted on a panel outside the ISS and exposed to the harsh conditions of space. The samples will then be returned to Earth, where Mahmooda and her team can study how they held up in space.

If SCOPE could be rated to withstand higher temperatures, however, it could fly closer to the sun and slingshot away even faster. Another NIAC Fellow, Artur Davoyan, has proposed **solar sails** that can skim near the sun to just a few times its radius. Such a path could zip a craft to Neptune in just 10 months!

Expanding the SCOPE

SCOPE is a small, low-**mass** craft. It does not need its own dedicated rocket for launch. Instead, SCOPE could hitch a ride into space aboard a rocket launching a larger spacecraft. Such an arrangement is called a *rideshare*. In addition, multiple SCOPE spacecraft could be launched at the same time. Mahmooda envisions several SCOPE's traveling to Triton to provide complete coverage of the moon.

Furthermore, the platform could be used to explore other targets in the outer **solar system** with the same advantages.

❝ It can be applicable to many targets including Uranus and Uranus's moons, the **Oort cloud,** and so on. ❞ —Mahmooda

SCOPE could reevaluate Pluto and capture more information about the side that was obscured during the flyby of the New Horizons spacecraft in 2015. SCOPE craft could travel to other known or suspected ocean worlds—including the moons Enceladus, Europa, Ganymede, and Titan—to gather more data about their ability to host life.

Illustration of a view of the dwarf planet Pluto from its moon Charon

Apart from being printed on a **solar sail,** the quantum dot spectrometer has a huge number of potential applications. Coupled with the falling cost of getting small satellites into orbit, such devices could used be in a constellation to track, among other things, the status of Earth's **atmosphere** and oceans—what started Mahmooda thinking about quantum dot spectrometers in the first place!

❚❚ It has many applications other than the specific mission architecture of SCOPE. ❚❚ —Mahmooda

Learning about exoplanets through the ice giants

SCOPE will do more than study the habitability of Triton. We can apply what SCOPE discovers about Uranus, Neptune, and their moons to planetary systems around other stars as well.

❝ Learning about Neptune and Triton could be really important for **exoplanet** studies. ❞ —Mahmooda

Extrasolar planets are planets that orbit around a star other than the sun. Astronomers have identified thousands of exoplanets. Many of these worlds have sizes, **masses,** and compositions similar to those of Uranus and Neptune. They could also have similar moons. If Triton is shown to have conditions that are favorable for life, it would greatly expand the search for life outside our **solar system.**

❝ So it could be really important to understand whether Triton could have life and how that relates to moons of exoplanets. ❞ —Mahmooda

Defying expectations

❝ A lot of the time, expectations are put on us by our family, our friends, our culture, our society that may not necessarily be best for us. ❞ —Mahmooda

❝ Once you decide what you're truly passionate about, don't let other people tell you what you can or cannot do. Just be persistent and keep sticking with your goal. ❞ —Mahmooda

Glossary

accelerate to change speed, to speed up.

aerospace the field of science, technology, and industry dealing with the flight of rockets and spacecraft through the atmosphere or the space beyond it.

atmosphere the mass of gases that surrounds a planet.

atom one of the most basic units of matter, consisting of a *nucleus* (core) of particles called *protons* and *neutrons* with tiny particles called *electrons* moving around the nucleus.

dwarf planet a rounded body orbiting the sun that does not have enough gravitational pull to clear other objects from its orbit.

engineer a person who uses scientific principles to design structures, such as bridges and skyscrapers, machines, and all sorts of products.

exoplanet (extrasolar planet) a planet that orbits a star other than the sun.

gravitational pull also called gravitation or the force of gravity, the force of attraction that acts between all objects because of their mass. Because of gravitation, an object that is near Earth falls toward the surface of the planet. We experience this force on our bodies as our weight.

ionosphere the part of an atmosphere that has many electrically charged particles.

Kuiper belt a region of icy objects in the outer solar system, beginning around the orbit of the planet Neptune. The Kuiper belt is also called the Edgeworth-Kuiper belt or the trans-Neptunian disk. An Irish scientist named Kenneth E. Edgeworth suggested in 1943 that the belt existed. The Dutch-born American astronomer Gerard P. Kuiper described it in more detail in 1951.

lander a spacecraft designed to land on a planet, moon, or other body in space.

mass the amount of matter something contains.

molecule two or more atoms bonded together.

momentum an object's force of motion. The momentum of a moving object equals its mass multiplied by its *velocity* (speed in a given direction).

nanotechnology the creation and study of structures that are slightly larger than atoms and molecules.

Oort cloud a cluster of comets and smaller objects in the outermost region of our solar system.

orbit a looping path around an object in space; the condition of circling a massive object in space under the influence of the object's gravity.

orbiter a spacecraft designed to orbit a planet or other object in space.

photon a tiny particle of light.

probe a rocket, satellite, or other uncrewed spacecraft carrying scientific instruments, to record or report back information about space.

propellant solid or liquid fuel that is turned into gas and put under pressure to push a spacecraft forward.

propulsion pushing something, such as a spacraft.

radiation energy given off in the form of waves or tiny particles of matter.

radiation pressure the force exerted by photons striking an object.

rover a lander designed to move about for surface exploration.

solar sail a large, lightweight structure designed to use the radiation pressure of sunlight to propel a spacecraft.

solar system the sun and everything that travels around it, including Earth and all the other planets and their moons.

Review and reflect

Now that you've finished reading about Mahmooda Sultana, use these pages to think about her experiences and SCOPE in new ways. As you work, reflect on the importance of creative problem solving, curiosity, and open-mindedness in life.

Complex problems and creative solutions

Why are scientists interested in studying Uranus and Neptune?

What are some of the problems associated with exploring the ice giants?

How does Mahmooda Sultana hope to overcome these challenges with ScienceCraft for Outer Planet Exploration (SCOPE)? What makes this solution so innovative?

Visit www.worldbook.com/resources to download sample answers, blank graphic organizers, and a rubric to evaluate writing.

Inspiration can come from anywhere!

Use a graphic organizer like the one below to map out your ideas. What ideas or experiences led to Mahmooda's innovative solution?

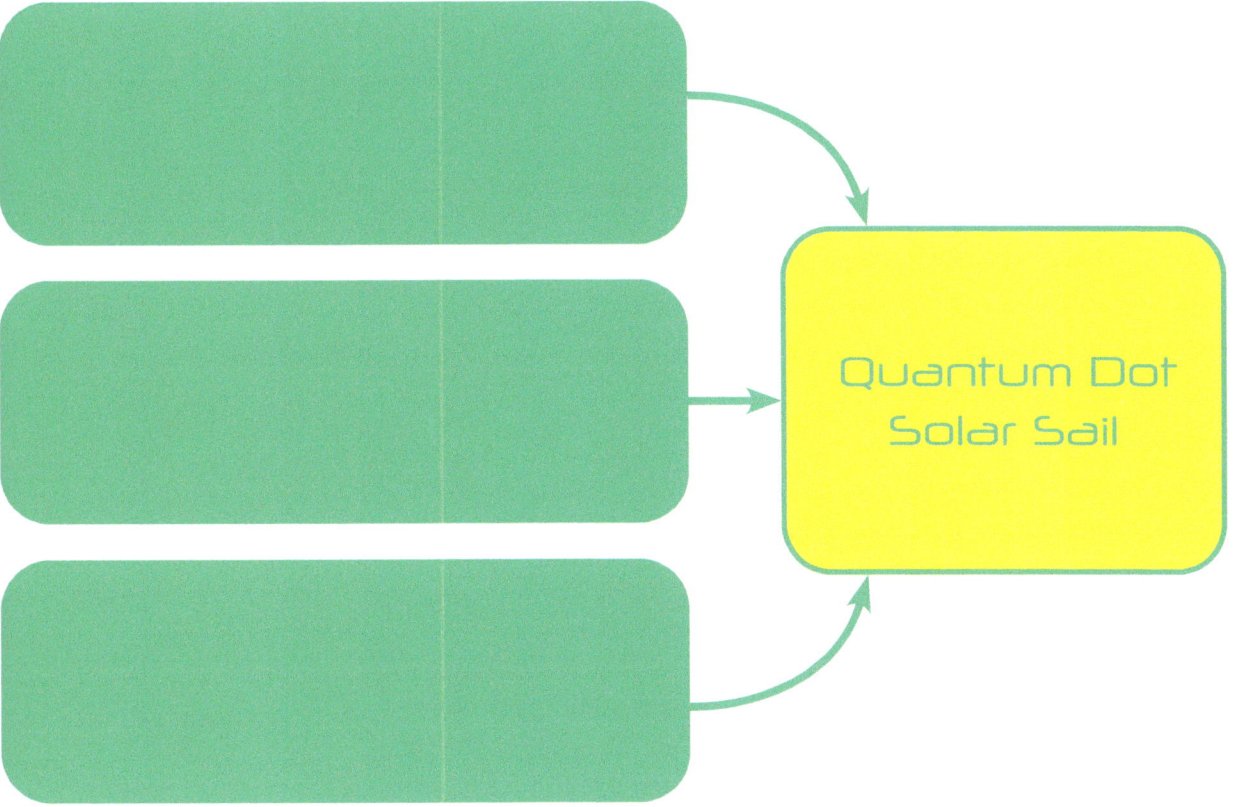

Write about it!

Think about Mahmooda's experiences in life and as a NIAC Fellow.

How has Mahmooda defied both social and engineering expectations? How can going against conventional wisdom help develop innovative solutions?

Index

A

atmosphere, 12-13, 18, 24-25, 41

B

Bawendi, Moungi, 27

C

Charon, 41
CubeSats, 26-27

D

Discovery Program (NASA program), 18
dwarf planets, 12, 41

E

electricity, 10-11, 13, 22, 28
Enceladus, 40
engineering, 10-11, 16-17
Europa, 40
exoplanets, 6-7, 18, 20, 42-43

F

flyby missions, 4, 12-15, 18, 40

G

Ganymede, 40
geysers, 14-15, 19
Goddard Space Flight Center (GSFC), 6, 32
gravity, 8, 12, 36
gravity assists, 8

H

helium, 24
hydrogen, 24-25

I

ice giants, 6, 12, 18, 42-43
International Space Station (ISS), 26, 38

Interplanetary Kite-craft Accelerated by Radiation of the Sun (IKAROS), 22-23
ionosphere, 13

J

Japanese Aerospace Exploration Agency (JAXA), 22
Jupiter, 8, 24

K

Kepler (telescope), 20
Kuiper belt, 12

L

LED TV's, 29
life (extraterrestrial), 8, 14, 40, 43
light, 20, 24-25, 27, 29-30

M

Mars, 4
Massachusetts Institute of Technology (MIT), 17, 27
Materials International Space Station Experiment (MISSE), 38
Mercury, 38

N

nanotechnology, 28-29
NASA Innovative Advanced Concepts program (NIAC), 7
NASA Outer Planets Assessment Group, 15
National Aeronautics and Space Administration (NASA), 7-8, 15, 18-19, 32
Neptune, 4, 8-9, 12-13, 18-19

O

oceans, 14-15, 40-41
Oort cloud, 40
optical transmission curves, 28, 30, 35

P

photons, 20, 36
pixels, 28, 35
Pluto, 12, 40-41
prisms, 27, 30

Q

quantum dots, 27-31, 34-35, 38, 41

R

radiation pressure, 20, 22, 36

S

Saturn, 8
ScienceCraft for Outer Planet Exploration (SCOPE), 34-36, 38-42
semiconductors, 28
solar sails, 22-23, 34-36, 38-39, 41
spectrometers, 24-27, 30, 34, 41
spectroscopy, 24-25
sun, 13, 22, 36-39

T

Titan, 8, 40
transmission curves. *See* optical transmission curves
Triton, 12-15, 18-19, 36, 42-43

U

ultraviolet radiation, 31
Uranus, 4-5, 8, 40, 42-43

V

Verne, Jules, 11
Voyager 1 (spacecraft), 8
Voyager 2 (spacecraft), 4-5, 8, 14-15, 19

www.ingramcontent.com/pod-product-compliance
Lightning Source LLC
Chambersburg PA
CBHW060934170426
43194CB00023B/2956